BLOOD SOAKED DRESSES

GLORIA MINDOCK

IBBETSON STREET PRESS

Cover photo: Laurie McGinley
Inside photo of Rufina Amaya: Laurie McGinley

ISBN: **978-1-4303-1034-1**
Library of Congress Control Number: 2007907912

IBBETSON STREET PRESS
25 SCHOOL STREET
SOMERVILLE, MA. 02143

617-628-2313

BLOOD SOAKED DRESSES

GLORIA MINDOCK

1/22/08

For my dear friend
Bill who is forever an
inspiration to me + my
favorite poet.
I hope you enjoy this book.
Much love ~
Glo

Acknowledgements

The author gratefully acknowledges the editors of the following publications where these poems first appeared, some in slightly different form.

UNU: Revista de Cultura: "Breathe," and "Dimness"

Indefinite Space: "Machine"

The Lyrical/Somerville News: "Walking in El Salvador," and "Glass Picture, Rosario Church, San Salvador"

Contemporary American Voices: "Dream For A Soldier"

Blackbox: "San Salvador, Looking Back Years Later," "El Mozote," and "Housecall"

Wilderness House Literary Review: "Charade"

Arabesques: "El Salvador, 1983," "Blood Soaked Dresses," "Oscar Romero," "Waiting For Execution," and "Knife"

Big Hammer: "Countryside Thoughts"

Murmur of Voices Anthology: "So Many Deaths Make Up the Face," and "Life Mourns"

Bagel With The Bards Anthology No. 1: "Life Mourns"

Bagel With the Bards Anthology No. 2: "Befallen"

With a very heartfelt thank you to Catherine Sasanov for her endless editing, years and years of friendship, and for always being there for me. I could not have done this without your help. My deepest gratitude to Dzvinia Orlowsky for her support of my writing and our many years of friendship. A thousand thanks as well to Flavia Cosma, Ioan Tepelea, Laurie McGinley, Tim Muth, Simon Perchik, John Minczeski, and Steve Glines for their comraderie and the many kindnesses they have shown me in so many different ways. Doug Holder, thank you for inspiring me daily, the many laughs and for publication of this book. And to my partner William J. Kelle: Thank you for the encouragement and support that you give me in all my writing endeavors.

For Mom, Dad, Kellis, Richard, Alexander, and Bill

This book is written in memory of Rufina Amaya, the only survivor of the massacre at El Mozote, El Salvador, where she witnessed her family and the people in her village, being murdered. In March, 2007, Rufina Amaya died of a stroke. She lived her life speaking about the atrocities committed so no one would forget. These poems are written in her honor, and in honor of all who died in El Salvador during the civil war from 1980-1992.

"But she had so rubbed her eyes from grief
that all she had seen could be seen in them."

THE MASSACRE AT EL MOZOTE
Mark Danner

TABLE OF CONTENTS

BLOOD SOAKED DRESSES

BLOOD SOAKED DRESSES

Death crawls underneath this world and waits. Who will be next?

Three months ago, the soldiers murdered my two little girls.
The bastards raped, tortured, and shot them in the head.
Their screams were like bad music replaying over and over in my
head. I talk to them every morning, and my day is planned for
me. At night, they invent my dreams. My daughters are in a
mass grave. Their blood soaked dresses engulf their exquisite
bones. They were so pretty. *Children, you were brave.*
You know the soldiers love was only fiction. Your scattered
brains now interview the earth and the earth speaks. For a little
while, I pretend they grew up. *I love this scenario.* Of course
reality sets in. The place I stay at is between the living and the
dead. Time stopped. Motionless, I hold my girls like a vine
twisting up into the heavens. *Alone, this gives me purpose ...*
living in a ceremony, a paradise. Such a beautiful day, feeling the
wind hit my face. I know it is a gift from the grave.

THE ATROCITIES

EL SALVADOR, 1983

Somewhere, someone is mourning
for the body of a brilliant one.
Man or woman, it doesn't matter.
The tears in this country, an entrance
to a void... shadows touching skin like frost.

A star fell north of this city. Armies parade around
in their uniforms bragging about the killings.
Dead bodies thrown into a pit, cry.
Flesh hits wind, wind hits flesh.
How many dead?
Finally, they are covered with dirt at noon.
All eyelids are closed.
No one knows nothing.
No breathing assaults to hold us. The bitter ash
weeps over the world, and no other country
wants to see it, taste
the dead on their tongue or wipe away all
the weeping.

LIFE MOURNS

Parents, you carry your children's coffins well.
Along the road, see the little gifts
left for you: blood stains, teeth, shoes.
The clouds gather up all the tears you cry
so everyone feels them when it rains.
The military buttons up its coats.

Children, you gather the bones of your parents quickly.
Identified by a piece of cloth, a shirt, a guess...
Sometimes you find bones at the front door, but never
where you hid. *You were lucky.*
But even you are the already dead
dying slowly from brutality.

Husband, body parts hang in the trees.
The Earth is sad today. Trees as sacred
as the lives of those whose hands,
heads, fingers, organs, eyes touch the branches
with their longing...
Husband, I know that you are on the first branch.

In this procession of sadness, I stand and console life.
Life, embarrassed, cries out to the Death Squads.
They do not hear.
Their ears are filled, and their hearts drowning.

EL MOZOTE

Bones on the side of the path
are collected, put into sacks.
I want to grab them. Empty them
on the ground and make a pattern.
How many sacks must I have to do this?
This is like playing pick-up sticks.
I could have the skull of my Mother, arm of a friend,
leg of my Father, and ribs of an unknown,
form them into a skeleton.
I have lived my life consuming these bones.
Arm loads for loving.

How gentle the sky looks today.
My vision is clear. Funny, how red the soil is.
Blood releases itself into a masterpiece.
A photographer takes a photo trying to open
the closed lips of the world.
Such speechless despair! When you look at the
pictures, will you wash yourself, feel your flesh,
sing a song, and live to remember?
Your life seems luxurious. Mine is strange,
empty like a shadow.
I see flowers form on the bullets as they ricochet
over me. When they hit someone, I see waves of dreams
never happening.

All these years, the knife gets deeper.
The machete gets quicker.
It floats in the air and crashes
into the living arms.
Hold tight this horror and weep.
Time will freeze the image.

EL SALVADOR BIRD WATCHES

Everyday parakeets flock over San Salvador at 5:00 AM and 5:00 PM

The wounds are not invisible. Hands, feet, and stomach all
chopped up with a machete, skin rotting.
This is a special delivery for the people.

My heart beats so fast into this shallow air.
How can I be heard?
Orange rinds are shoved into my mouth
suffocating me with fragrance. Sadness engulfs me
to know my skin will be stripped and added to the heap.

Such emotion the stench brings
knowing the ripeness is a different existence floating by.
The soldiers behead all who stay.
The parakeets look down and land in my blood
cleaning it up.
The sky is blue, and it's just another day.
The birds peck at the worms and bite off.

WAITING FOR EXECUTION

My spirit accelerated into the sky.
The mountains were happy by the sea.
The enemy was not around.

At church, communion was red wine. A sip—I wanted
it all. To drink would make my life last, make me immune.
God of God, this air is hot.
I'm heaving from the stench. These are the bodies
in your hands. How many can you hold?
Will you hold me?

I'm dreaming of saving my memories.
I close the window and lay on the floor.
If I play invisible, they will murder God and not me.
God, they hate you, want you in a cage like a dog,
leaving me in limbo, seeking you. A catastrophe.

This pain waits for an entrance.
If they shoot me, I conquer, and you God,
unseen in your cage, cry, escaping from my rusted dreams.

ARCHBISHOP ROMERO

Sin has formed on their mouths, and they
assault us.
We are silenced into a void.
Souls singled out for torture.

Oscar Romero created a heaven,
carried us in his arms of prayer.
In church, we drink Christ to free ourselves.
Decapitation was not a devotion to believe in.
The soldiers will burn in a red sky.

When Oscar gave his life to the Lord,
he made a bed of blood and bones, turned it
into a path of purity so white that only the people
of El Salvador could use it. Sometimes we flee
on horseback to get away from the visible.

We learned to deliver our ashes and rise
up. Bury ourselves in this white
church with a bullet to our bone.
Scorched from the hot sun, our sandals
fall apart. We carry ourselves like a surge, proud
and capable of waiting for our execution.

Oscar was married to the church.
Life was only his bride for awhile.
He is the altar we pray at diligently.
We pray our dreams are received
as they assassinate us kneeling.
Better to die this way than clinging
to the wrong light. The soldiers are like wild animals.
A bite that shows such commotion that we laugh.

GLASS PICTURE, ROSARIO CHURCH, SAN SALVADOR

So many things break apart our lives.
Irreparable, we move on.
When I said good-bye to you, you were in
the coffin. Only your face shown under glass—
a window for memory.
You sleep now in peace.
My tears fall. If I put my lips to the glass, will it fog up?
Will I lose sight of your face?
Will I pretend that the soldiers never killed you,
that you're drifting into a place
I can't find?
If I try to hear you, will you still talk to me?
How will I get by without your thoughts?
I pray you will receive me as I
lean towards your casket.

CAMPESINOS

Their skin is tough
with eyes soft and tender.
Campesinos speak with words
so powerful and no apology.
Houses are gone,
dolls left on the side of the road,
San Miguel is draped in ashes, silence...
All hope gone, alone.

There is a scar left that sings,
all the pictures can't capture
what took place.
Heaven is barefoot.
How can you show hell?

The American government said the atrocities
were "communist propaganda."
Tell that to the Campesinos and the survivors
who witnessed the thirst of knives.

Their sorrow gathers together,
darkness spreads.
Here, they cry, break down, tremble
with pain in solitude.

KNIFE

I am in pieces.
I close my eyes, cry slowly as
to not flood myself.
A storm happens and my body
is everywhere.
I pick up my bones, heart, teeth, hair.
I make a column of them and sleep underneath.
You will not find me.
Rest, my love, darkness has defeated you.
An abyss surrounds you, and I conclude, it
was always like this.

I am wounded—
You aren't.
We exist separately forever.
Me, with my searching…
You, with your dead blood, your murdered
heart wandering in the dark—
faceless and rootless.
No light to guide your motion.
Bitter taste in your mouth.
Forget that you can kiss and smell your hand.

WALKING IN EL SALVADOR

I travel this night single with the quiet streets
tapping at the heel of my shoe.
So much pain coming from these buildings.
People are living on their rosary.
Reciting prayers to our Lord in hidden silence.

Sin can be a paradise if you let it.
I tumble into this dark night reaching for
some purity.

A man is standing on a corner smoking
a cigar. I want to speak to him, open up with a strangeness
that will levitate this block.
This place is sadder than I am.

I travel this night single with the wind gently
touching my face. I continue to walk and say nothing.

COUNTRYSIDE THOUGHTS

COUNTRYSIDE THOUGHTS

Sometimes when I see the stars, I wish they'd fall. Such
streaks of light in a hurry to hit the ground. Like my heart,
they turn to stone. Sometimes, there is no time to do what
I want. Sometimes, well mostly, the government doesn't
let me do what I want. Living here just drowns my eyes.
So many who speak are killed. Erasable. Everything is
bleeding here. You have to die in heaps of flesh to have a
cleanup. Strangers, enjoy your alternatives. Live your life
awake. You never know when a throbbing pulse will take
over political parties, military men who love red splashed
across their bodies. Float in your freedom. Whistle some.
Blow me a kiss from across the world. Without this, the
dawn would pierce me, pinning me down into the fallen
leaves. I need not feel burdened. I need to push my
dreams into the day, and watch those in charge crumble.
The disappeared do not become drink for the thirsty earth
for nothing. I'm stretched out on a chair, hoping to live
one more day in this countryside, enjoying the fragrance
instead of dealing with the whispers of horror. Today,
I would lift my wings, *if I had them*, up into the heavens.

BEFALLEN

"SOMETIMES, WHEN I AM ANGRY IT SEEMS
I COULD START MY OWN COUNTRY."
Steve Masor

The one last heart to remain in
this world circles around me.

Angel, I have a good perspective about this.
A heart is on my doorstep, and it is haunting,
figuring out who it will go to.
I have courage. The dead love me.

My bleached white heart. Polished
for the breaking. Splintering for the hell of it.
You figure it out.

Should I start my own country?
Build my own constellation? Something
to be stared at in the night?

If I take the unknown, it might have a sin I can't live with—
could be risky. That heart longs for a gaze
but just gets an ending
stopping short of a song.

Angel, I am devoted.
Bury me in your wings.
Enfold me for safe-keeping.
I need to be warm.

SO MANY DEATHS MAKE UP THE FACE

The Angels are ready to increase their depth.
My face is hollow—
They're digging into the skull until I
can't tell life from death, death from life.
Angels wrap themselves around me
tightening their grip to bone
until the heart is all that is left to be seen, blood red
and beating. Pumping itself confused.
It wants a shoulder, wants to stick to my ribs,
but there is nothing to stick to.
The Angels took care of that. All there is,
is this eternity of waiting
until dust is only a dream.

CHARADE

I'm making up the light today.
You could never understand
the water in my veins.

Angel, face me. At least give me
an illusion of love.
This heart is between life,
between death,
between voices.
Like a wave,
I want to break and let you
cover me with clouds.

Angel, swing my pain,
reverse this judgment.
In my life, you have only tapped
my shoulder. An error.
Bizarre and weeping, you drown me.
Dreaming, I thought the world was
a corridor. I was wrong.
You've taken everything away. It's eerie.
All this dying unseen.
All this upside down walking.
On and on I stay put.

Oh Angel, I won't talk now.
Your air passes through me.
It's true, I know now: this is a charade
thought out carefully by your arms.
I am nothing but a landscape.
Abused.
A village for others to travel through
in parts of the day.

BREATHE

I can hear the dead breathing on me
from heaven.
Their exhales tickle my skin,
a soft paint brush.
Are they trying to change my existence or
their own?

Hoping for flesh, heart, voice, and tongue, they try
to make my speech a patchwork
for their freedom.
I got used to them—started to smoke Camels
and totally enjoyed our barriers.
Each of us alone, shaken and sleeping
into our own need, waits like a flower
or a bug growing out of time.

SEEING IS ONLY A FLAWED SECRET

I imagine what death will be like—
A long shadow filling my body.
The air hopeless in its attempt to revive me.

I have conversations with the abyss.
My weary mind is just a symbol. No voice
comforts me. Illness hits, a red knife
sinking into flesh. The coffin is quick.
My anguish is a secret crucified.

The sky is gray today,
healing itself back to blue.
Gazing at me: arms, legs, eyes...
consuming me like a wolf, building its own domain.
This is an injustice. Surviving war but not a disease
good for a ritualistic slaughter.

How generous this life! It teases you, rocks you,
loves you, caresses you, and then attacks you
with terror.
Jesus, rearrange your schedule.
God, show me your lips. Make your kiss
a compass so I know where to go.

I look out the window and feel
like a fool.
Everyone carries on with no ears.
Such motionless supervision—a crime!
They roam, I roam, we all roam.
Too many shoes pounding this earth...
faces torn out of life...effigies, I crave.

Death is a prophet. It sips my blood slowly, feeding on me.
With angelic speed and prayer, I will wipe it
from my body.

24

DIMNESS

Blood spurts out—
each star bleeding dry
until it shrivels up,
falls to its death.

The light shining from them
was a sign of surrender,
quietness, and waiting.

I wait,
my heart drenched and drowning,
gulping for thought,
for one last breath before
stopping.

I surrender.
I, too, have fallen.
Who will hold me
in their hand, give me
a transfusion?

HOUSECALL

Heard your voice in my sleep
while you hammered thorns
into my skin.
When you touched my hand, my blood
felt perfect, paralyzed.
I choked on a word
but couldn't pronounce it. It still weighs
heavier than me. A thickness
of red covering my mouth.

What is this space I've been occupying?
A shadow which melts
into making me terminal.
Drifting away from memories, I need
to go deeper—
stray away from the death that
keeps me strapped.

EL JEFE

The stars will not fall for you.
Nothing to make a wish on—
Your thoughts spin,
trying to find gravity but instead
infinity, infinity, infinity.

Aloneness suits you.
Your family will not attach themselves.
Hearts circle but do not stop.
What will you do with all your fame
and good looks?

Like a wolf eating flesh,
you devour all the pages.
You just kill and survive,
let your name live
inside your head.

If you have tears, they never come.
The insides of you never answer.

DANCING

My shadowed heart
you should feel love,
but you do not understand
the luminous
nor the dreams that clatter.
I saw them full of flight

over the village weeping
and over a pressed passion. I sacrificed
and ruined my world.
Out of all this glorious
suffering, my temples clump and horrify me.

I love those gleaming eyes.
Let my pain entangle your brow
outspread and silent.

A beautiful image—
our world and my fierce dancing
for glitter.

TORMENT

Swimming in a stream of nothingness,
there is no line
to grab me.
My speech comes out in a scream.

Must I wrestle with these borrowed dreams?
Convince myself of song?
Do I really have the gift of breath?
Tongue is cursing throat—
Fingers flicker out—
Eyes desire teeth—
Life of the petrified dead
remind me of my torment.

I fear turning pale
with pastures above me,
green and abundant.
A shadow fell on me—
A spell at birth,
ugly and perishing.
26 years later, nothing has changed
and I am running out of ruins.

El Salvador is crazy.
It has abandoned me and blessed me
with nightfall.

DEATH MARCH

No one came to pay respects.
Father Miguel released you in ceremony.
It was his job.

Striking a match and lighting a candle,
the flame reminds me
of a reflection of myself
I saw in a window:
blank with no eyes—
I was tempted to nod, but someone might see.

The flowers here are many.
I sent the white ones.
My fingers touch their petals and I
pretend to see you laughing.
You always did carry on with
such emotion.
Our hands always insisted
on hurling our thoughts into each other—

My automatic life is empty
imagining myself where you are.
Exhausted, I need to sleep.

If I am able to remain in love, know this:
I will scream into infinity.

Who will be at my funeral?
Who out of this dying world?
A few friends, family, a pair of eyes that loved me
but never told me—

Let us sleep admired.

A DRY GRAVE

The ugly people
desiccated like mummies
possess this water:
Pink, smooth, sudsy.

They create a state of frenzy.

Their revenge
reddens like wine.
A dictator's delight
to flow blood from nails.

Their enamel bites.
There is a story to tell,
but the population is resigned.

No hope this day,
No place can they
go except to drink
from a nothingness.

HEARTS

HEART

I try to think the way you do,
to forget the way you do—
My mind murmurs with every
confession.

Forgive me but I'm
trembling for the morning.
The night still burns me:
breathless.
Every night, the yard, the stars—
every tree fully heightened,
fully dead.

Where is my dog? Where are my brothers, my sisters,
my parents, my friends?

A lust for home pushes me back
into the delicate place I've built here.
I want to sleep in the past but I believe
this living is gesture.

BILLBOARDS

I'll never be able to share
what I just saw.
The red light was blazing.
It was an act of murder
trembling as it crushed out
the sky.
I need a reflection and one minute
of your hand resting gently
on my shoulder, warming my failures
into an advertisement.
At the outskirts of the city,
I step on the gas faster and faster
until my life is merely links—
a translucent house
where love stands expressed.

EL COMANDANTE

A figure gradually trembling
over the years,
I've been a monster touching
out into the street.

When I look at the stars
it's no accident.
I will sacrifice and become
a body—
A memory
smoothing over your mouth,
tender and purposeful.

I realize now the threads
I bear are sisterly,
neutral,
blurred.
It is time to be part of
the crowd
like a painting
looked at forever.

DREAM FOR A SOLDIER

Jesus, with blood-filled tears,
exiles me to my dreams.
There is no word for me
not seized by language.

Soldier, in this silence I see a vision
which cuts out your sweaty heart.
You are fearful, cold, plunged
into panic.
One dream after another, this replays and is
documented.

Jesus, this is not sorrowful and this
is not torture. This is only me, holding
his heart under water.

Jesus, you will not answer his prayers.
Just give him a scrap not wished for.
Tease him once in awhile
with a beating heart.
Scrub him with intoxication.
Let him hope.

I

In how many languages can I
say it until you take me seriously?
The volumes in my head aren't
narrative or comfortable.
I can't recreate anymore agonies.
My score has long since been up.

Do you know what I do all day?
Do you know what you will become?
It is all a surrender.
I need just one moment of consolation.
You need to be happy with me—
to know what spring is.

It is early morning now.
It is difficult not to weep.

Have a conversation with me.
Plop it into your chest.
We are everything to each other, a separation
by dust, with every night kissing us
into recognition.

EXILE

LEAVING MY COUNTRY

My heart curls up into a ball
and is silent.
Exhausted, my hopes only
have a miniature glow.
What you did was uncalled for.

My thoughts will crush
your popularity and explode
your esophagus.
No one will understand you.
How bittersweet this will be.

My heart spreads out and warms my body—
delicately.
Now, I light a candle and sit,
caressing a laugh.

ENDLESS

You blend in and what comes out are
sounds.
No one cares to understand
the face of things.
This is your last time to laugh.
Check out all the exit signs and arrive
in Paris.

The stillness engulfs you like prison.
The life lines show in your skin.
No beauty here.
Even your heart vanishes, burns
you to ash…to specks…to darkness
even the wind doesn't want.

Endless fire burning you down.
Too bad.

SOLDIER

I put flowers on imaginary graves.
Especially since I don't know
where the bodies are.

I resent your brutality.
My lips are destroyed.
Skin hangs from my bones, but
still you try to kiss me.
This torture has its advantages—
It reminds me that death is my only warmth.

My wounds are superficial.
I control my words with quietness
which betrays my blood, which wants to escape
from this body and scream with its own voice.

Tell me what you want.
The hourglass is empty.
Forget it, I'll endure.
I will try to sleep when you leave.
I did not bargain for this.
I am hurt, and I am searching for a halo.
In my thoughts, I'm laughing
as the world dissolves.

FALLING

Hmmm...
My life is like a
soaked leaf—
Chaotic.
Ghostly trees
sway toward the ground
occasionally fierce.

It is dark.
No one sees.
There is the dampness
of arms sliding upward—
Uncontrollable—
This ride—

The noise says
I am still searching for
a muddy bed.

DEATH DANCE

There are no words for suffering.
It has many faces—
too many to separate.

Living this way gives a strange weariness that
has swept my voice, my dreams, away.
The angels haven't been playing
trumpets lately.
Silence is all I hear.

A cold blackness dances into my muscles.
Such soft little paws arranging their touch
into drum beats.
I am not prepared for this telegraph.

Fate is retribution for being born.
How many times can I be opened up,
sewn back together?
There are pieces of me already drifting
into infinity.

Please give me some mercy,
a break from shivering.
This interrogation is bringing on tears,
torture like a sunset that
slowly turns to black
over and over
feasting on my dawns.

I must sew my body back
together like a garden.
Piece by piece watered and tended to
until a flower appears.

Someday, I won't be sluggish.
I'll be able to take your hand and tell you
who I really am.
Right now the bitter executioner condemns me.
Soldiers fire.
My nerves are shot.

When I don't return, open the trunk I keep.
Everything in there has a wing,
thoughts escaping
on the icons I kept.

FEEDING

What a combination!
The worse it is, the more the flow.
Battle after battle, season after season,
I grow up with stones.
Each year my voice feeds on knives,
mad for someone to listen.

I would like to believe my exile
is over, and the rays of the sun
will unfold my eyes.
What is there to see?
Is it serious?
Is it silent?
Is this where I die never knowing
the height of my brain?
The doom and coldness welcomes me,
a core of life just dreamed, pursued
by an empty stream where I drown with
the fish asking for love.

STORY

This is not pleasant—
we are both victims.

The rest of our friends talk sadly now.
My friend, my dear friend, your gentleness
is always upon me.
Your spirit: my moral essence.
This is not a lovely day.

I miss you, our combination
of realism and sentimentalism—
afraid of snow and afraid of
a candle flame—a reminder
of celebrated glory.
Losing you like this
makes you the ultimate angel
and me: waiting for dinner.

I am too good, too sensitive, too nice to live.

MONUMENT

I slip into the corridor almost
invisible.
No one notices.
Where will my next location be?

Everything always happens so fast—
You nail me to the sunlight.
Look at me like you look
out of windows.

I have had some existence:
dreams and exhaustion.
If anything is important, it is moments
catching wind on our faces,
dwindling away the afternoon.

We can squeeze the rain
in our hands.
Enchanted by this, we hear
a thousand voices singing:
the sound measuring us
for another
day, drifting...

Is it too much for you?
There is no map to follow.
Explain to me why I am invisible.
Only then can I have memories
which are in command.

MESH

I don't dare stay awake or feel
my heart beat vacancy
into freedom.

Someday, I will ask God
to sing to me.
He will smile and change
my touch into directions of green,
into wind, buried...

rain stretching out
beyond the equator...

a new horizon, tickled.

I drift into sickness.
I am a branch,
a procession,
a voyage slumbering
into hum.

WOLF

Every hour a new one elected
Still no word
A look, a suffering, a love
to keep outsiders out

As light bulbs trace
this guard of personal
handling
this possessiveness

Sometimes we all sit
in a circle
hovering
The trespasser must be sought

Every second the crying of a wolf
emerges inside one of us

LOOKING BACK

EITHER

Was I provoked or just
deposited into this world?
All the material printed gives
no answer and makes me believe
no one is magnificent.
I wasted time being.
The public bombards me with theatrics.
I watch everyone
perform the obvious.
I guess war is necessary,
economy for the living.

REMEMBRANCE

I visit the graveyards and think
strange thoughts, chant little songs, and wonder
if all the bones have disintegrated
into dust yet.

I want to bring a bone back with me,
have it tell me its story.
What sort of human it nestled in,
the sickness it felt, and if it ever was broken.

I would listen to the sorrow
the dead feel, their greatest happiness...

I would bring home bone after bone
(one bone per human)
searching for the ultimate perfect life.
But there are limits to the silence between words.
The whole graveyard turns
into an annual report.
Notebooks of lives lived.
One woman wanted a man in her coffin
for companionship. Another was disappointed,
thought sunsets would be brighter dead.
Another screamed her life away,
but no one listened.
The bones tell it all.

When I die, I want the perfect story
to be told by my bones.
Comparing myself alive, I will make sure
I have memories.
When my bone is picked up, I can be remembered.

SAN SALVADOR: LOOKING BACK

You are suspended as a cloud only once.
This is where you seek battles, taste
death, and invent situations with
the emptiness of your tongue.

Embrace yourself. There is no guarantee
of a complete death.
Your heart has been transplanted
into the necessary. Your kiss will not last long.
Solitude will be your witness.
It was all a strange conspiracy,
stretched out and mad.

I went for a walk today. It changed me.
Where the road led was striking.
Too many body parts crucified.

I sip a cup of coffee and bury you
in its heat. Each sip an embalming.
Seeing your face, I know we are chained
by our own hands digging in the dirt.

FIXED

I could let go and be
surrounded by air—
No brutality or obscene marks
just achievement.

I will not cry to exquisite hearts—
They like me.
My reputation shakes
into seductive streets, soft doorways.
What a set-up.
A marvelous collection of soldiers
conveying love—

The kind of revolution you
want to imagine—
Not what I have now.
Oh, such a tiresome law.

We move quickly—
It's cold, and the dead read aloud here—
a melodrama, eerie...

HOPE

Everything means something to me.
I store my own leaves
of darkness
so don't worry.
Death moves at incredible speed
but I move faster,
so fast in fact, that the boundaries between us
can only dream.

Sometimes I forget this.
The air is windows
and I tap my hand waiting
for the invisible, when life
and death meet on the curving
line, and I favor one.

ABOUT THE AUTHOR

Gloria Mindock is the editor of Červená Barva Press and the online journal, *Istanbul Literature Review.* She is the author of two chapbooks, *Doppelganger* (S. Press) and *Oh Angel* (U Šoku Štampa). Her second full-length collection of poems, *Nothing Divine Here*, is forthcoming from U Šoku Štampa as well. A winner of a Massachusetts Cultural Council grant in poetry, she lives in Somerville, Massachusetts, where she freelances editing manuscripts and conducting workshops for writers.

ABOUT THE PHOTOGRAPHER

Laurie McGinley has a strong connection to Latin America and believes that photographs have a unique power to evoke emotions, memories and feelings that have been long buried. As Altagracia, a former Salvadoran guerilla, said, "Looking at these photos is like tuning into a time that we can no longer hear." Laurie McGinley's work can be found at www.lauriemcginley.com

COLOPHON

This book was designed by Steve Glines. Headline fonts are Copperplate Gothic, text is Maiandra GD.